Grace
The Brenda Lee Eager Story

From Behind The Starting Line

A Memoir & Pictorial

Brenda Lee Eager

Printed and Bound in the United States of America
Published and Distributed by:
Professional Publishing House
1424 W. Manchester Ave., Suite B
Los Angeles, CA 90047
www.professionalpublishinghouse.com
Drrosie@aol.com
323-750-3592

Cover Design: Clark Graphic Images

Formatting: Alpha Enterprises

First Printing, March 2011

10 9 8 7 6 5 4 3 2 1

ISBN 978-0-9826704-9-1

Publisher's Note

Dedication

This book is dedicated to my daughter Michelle who told me to write my story for my Grand-children. It is also for Corey Anthony and Quinton Anthony and your children. For all of the people who have helped me to grow through the years. For those of you Aunts and Uncles, Cousins, Dear Friends, who encouraged me to keep going when it sometimes seemed hopeless. To all of my ten sisters and brothers that I grew up with, Consulia Jr, Mary Lee, Dorethia, CC, Kenneth, Alvin, Timothy, John, Debra Ann, and Willie even though you are on the other side you are here in my heart, for I can see you dancing whenever I close my eyes.

Table of Contents

Table of Contents

Acknowledgements

Thank you to all of my co-writers down through the years. Chuck Jackson, it started with you! "If It's Real What I Feel" was my first record with Jerry Butler. Bob Boogie Bowles, it was fun being young and determined to be great songwriters with you. Billy Osborne, you can catch a groove that will shake the dead. Thank you for the music, Marcel East, writing with you is a spiritual experience. Ben Dowling, it's so much fun. Steven Bray, Al McKay, whew! What grooves! What Joy!

Prince, I have always been a fan and to have co--written some songs with you is just crazy! Thank you is an understatement!

Carey Gordy and Bruce Fisher, I loved those times and those songs. Zoe Fox, Oliver Roullion, Hilliard Wilson, Vaughn Despenza and Gino Finley, it was so much fun. To Larry Ball and Alex Brown, I am determined to "LET GOD BE GOD" in my life. Todd Hunter, you are "More Than Beautiful." To every one else, I thank you for your music that married my lyrics and melodies, to help me to tell my stories, I'm forever grateful!

Thank you Jesse and Jacqueline Jackson, and Operation Breadbasket that included my sisters, 'The

Piperettes', Sue Conway, Pat Henley, and Delores Scott--we were there and we will tell our story.

And a special thank you to Mr. Ray Charles and my Sis Teena Marie. Love you both, forever. Thank you to all of my singing friends, I love singing with you all. I also truly send a special thank you to all who have helped me along the way--with your love, kindness, nourishment and protection. I appreciate and love you all.

To Mrs. Rolaneese Bradley, wherever you are I love you. To my Spiritual mentors I love and appreciate you, Rev. Linda Logan, Rev. Michael Beckwith, Rev OC Smith and everyone who helped me to grow into me. To my dear parents Consulia and Willie Dell Eager and to all of my ancestors whose shoulders I stand upon. And thank you to Pam Woodlief-McCullough for her tireless work and editorial intelligence, I really appreciate you. And to dear Dr. Rose Milligan, who came out of retirement to publish this book. Wow, I can't thank you enough. God bless you all. I love you.

Thanks to Kenn Goldstein for your inspiration. Terrah Bennett Smith, the Director of "Grace," thank you for your hard work. Akuyoe Graham, thank you for the beginning. To all of my singer and musician friends-- Can't do what I do without you. Love you CC

Bass, Terry Young, Della, Will, Fred, Theresa, Bridgette and all of the rest of you. That covers everyone. I Love you! I love God! I love Life!

About The Author

BRENDA LEE EAGER was born BRENDA MARIE EAGER in Mobile Alabama, August 6, 1947, she is the oldest of eleven children born to Willie Dell and Consulia Harris Eager. She attended Monroe Jr. High School in lower Peachtree, Alabama. She started singing in church and at school, but it was her ninth grade teacher Mrs. Bradley that told her that she was also a writer after reading some of her short stories.

She graduated from Blount High School in Prichard Alabama and started singing professionally at the Kings Club before going to New York to further pursue her career from New York From New York to marriage and a daughter named Michelle, who is now married to a Paul and have two Grandsons that are young musicians and singers also. Brenda traveled to Chicago, then to Los Angeles where she currently resides. She has recorded hit songs with the legendary Jerry Butler, Ray Charles and others, as well as being solo artist for Phonogram Mercury, Playboy Record, and Private Eye Records. She has written songs for Mavis Staples, Bobby Womack, Shirley Brown. She has written songs for Mavis Staples, Bobby Womack, Shirley Brown. Gwen Mccrae, Cliff Richards, Prince and more. She performed with Donny Hathaway, Roberta Flack, Smokey Robinson, Diana Ross, Gladys Knight, Graham Nash, Teena Marina and others. She continues to travel the world singing, writing, doing vocal and songwriting empowering others to be who they are and dare to live their dreams, she currently is performing 'GRACE THE BRENDA LEE EAGER STORY" her life, her songs. Brenda Lee encourages us all to Live, Love and laugh a lot!

Where It All Started

I was born in Saint Martin de Porres Hospital, in Mobile Alabama, on August 6, 1947. I really think that I remember my birth, myself. *Do you ever think that you remember your birth?* It was raining hard on that hot August night. Everything was happening on the second floor of the red brick building that had beautiful stained glass windows of Mary, Jesus' mother. Each time the lightning flashed, it lit up the windows to the hospital room. There was a tree waving its limbs and crashing against the window as if it was trying to break the glass. In the *wee* hours of the morning, Ma'dear was lying on a gurney, all of 19 years old, writhing in pain. No! She was *wallowing* in pain. She cried out, "Oh, lawdy, somebody help me!" No one came, even though she could hear them right outside the hospital door. All of a sudden, her cries became desperate as she wailed, "Somebody help me; please don't let my baby fall on the floor!" Immediately, there were three nurses in the room, *all* white *in* white. They looked down and there I was,

12

between my mommas legs, screaming like a Banshee. Nurse Gretchen, the head nurse, was a big blond woman who walked like an army sergeant. She was angry for having had been disturbed, but faked a smile and said to Ma'dear, "Why Mrs. Eager, you've got yourself a little girl. So they laid my naked, screaming butt on my Ma'dear's chest. I was now born.

The next day my Aunt Gladys, Daddy's only sister, came to the hospital...drunk.

"Umm, she don't look like her daddy, but can I name her?"

Ma'dear said "Okay Gladys, what will you name her?" Now Aunt Gladys looked puzzled as if she was trying to think. She then had an "ah ha" moment and proudly said,

"I am naming her Brenda-Marie-Joyce-Sue-Carolyn-Ann Eager!"

My grandmother Corinne, Ma'dear's mother, was so dis-pleased by Aunt Gladys' appearance and loud behavior, and she was rolling her big brown eyes at Aunt Gladys. Grandma was a kind, but stern, woman and took no bull. She was a "stout" woman with reddish brown skin and black hair. Her features made her look like a Samoan. She spoke and firmly said to Aunt Gladys, "Gladys, you will not be naming my grandchild all them names! The child won't know what to answer to! So pick out two and we will do away with the rest of them. And I mean it!" I became

13

Brenda Marie Eager. Ma'dear told me that I did not grow any hair on my head until I was three years old -- bald headed me!

By the time I was three, I had two sisters, Mary Lee and Dorethia. I was regularly singing at family gatherings and had now started singing at church. The first song I remember performing was "You don't have to be a soldier in a uniform." It was an old spiritual song that I performed with all of my heart and soul.

I went to kindergarten in Mobile where my Aunt, Annie Sikes Packer, was my teacher. She was married to my daddy's "'Uncle Sweet Baby" and even today I don't know Uncle Sweet Baby's real name. He has since passed away. We attended school in the little red school house that Uncle Sweet Baby had built when his children were little. Aunt Annie would hit us on the hand with a ruler, pinch us when we got an answer wrong or spank us if we had been unruly during school time. It seemed to me that I got a lot of pinches. But when the time came, I was so glad to graduate from kindergarten. It was very meaningful for my entire family, even though I did not know that my life was about to change, drastically.

The Move

I found out later that it was Ma'dear who wanted to move back to the country to be near her parents. So in order to please her, Daddy packed us up and moved us to Lower Peachtree, Alabama, about sixty miles from Selma, Alabama and about one hundred twenty miles from Mobile.

He rented the house and land that was next to my Grandparents and commenced to be a farmer. Daddy was fresh out of the Marines, but swore that he was going to raise lots of children and be a great farmer, like my Granddad. That rivalry started then! He was well on his way with the child raising. The children now consisted of me, Mary Lee, Dorethia, and Consulia Jr. Four children in four years and another one on the way.

We lived in an "l" shaped three room house, they used to call shotgun shacks, with a kitchen in the back and a back door that lead to the yard where we would go to get water from the red water pump.

When we first moved in, there was no electricity. But, we had it put in before I turned seven. We also had a wood burning stove that was replaced by an electric stove around the same time. But, at the age of six, I learned how to cook on the wood stove. We later got a gas stove and had a huge gas tank in the back yard to supply the gas. This was necessary because we were so far from the city. We had one wood- burning fireplace in the front room where we would all gather in the winter to keep warm. There was a pond at the edge of the property that separated our farm from the Jacksons, and the pond had catfish in it and lots of frogs, snakes and tadpoles. We would wade through the water and splash around it for fun.

Something Within Us Knows

O ne day when he was three years old, my brother, Consulia Jr., was in the kitchen with Ma'dear and picked up a jar of liquid. Thinking that it was water, he drank it down. Ma'dear saw him retch as he started vomiting. In that moment, she knew that he had drunk the kerosene that she used to light the fires on the stove. He was convulsing and turning blue, and knowing that there was no doctor around, I saw my mother calm down, lift her hands to the sky and quietly say, "Lawd, please show me what to do to save my child."

She calmly went to the cupboard, pulled out a can of lard and started to pack it into Jr's mouth. He really started vomiting again, but the lard had clumped around the kerosene and was bringing it out. She then made him drink a lot of water as the rest of us were crying not knowing what was happening to our little curly-headed brother. He was so tired and weak by then that he just lay in my mother's arms. She softly hummed and said, "Thank you Jesus."

First Grade

I loved my first grade teacher. Her name was Beulah Packer, a pretty, petite brown- skinned woman who sang and played piano. I still remember how she would place her fingers on the piano and when she hit the keys she would raise her fingers almost up to her face. To this day, I have never seen anyone play like her. I started to learn about musical instruments from her and the notes on the piano. Sometimes I would go home with her for a night and she would cook the best sweet potato pudding! Ooooweee! I can still taste them! She and her husband would later die in one of the worst car accidents in our community. Both of their daughters were thrown from the car and survived. I sometimes still grieve for her.

I had two best friends, Amanda Gates (we called Mandy Bett) and Mary Helen Packer, who would remain my best friends through the ninth grade. We use to take the big yellow school bus to school. Mr. Brooksie Tate would drive up to Lamberts Quarters. That's what they called the part of Peachtree that we lived in. It was named after a white overseer who lived there years before and owned a lot of the land. It was so far off the beaten path from the main road. The bus would pick us up from Bells Chapel Baptist Church at the bottom of a steep hill on my Grand-father's land. All of the neighborhood kids would gather there at seven thirty in the morning to be picked up and taken to Packers Bend, to the school. There was a tall oak tree standing in the fork of the road where the bus driver would come and turn around. If the other kids in the area weren't under that tree, he would leave, and it was a good ten miles or so to the school. Sometimes in the winter it would be so cold that we would build a fire under the tree to keep warm while we waited for the bus. We would put the fire out just before it came. It's no wonder we did not start a big fire. The fire would have had to jump across a lot of gravel to get to the other trees and farm land.

The bus would travel up the winding hills and curves. Kids would scream and run up and down the aisle as Mr. Brooksie would scream at us children all the way to school.

"Sit down little chillen! I said sit down little chillen, ya'll are so unruly!" Our stop was the last stop before school, so all of the kids would be excited to see one another. "Sit down, chillen'! I aint driving this $#@% bus next year!" He would really get nervous when we came to the Holy Branch. He would make us sit down and not say a word. We would obey. We were all afraid of the Holy Branch. It was a creek of deep water with a worn out bridge that creaked and shook when we drove over it. We all know of the tragedy that had taken place at the Branch just the previous year. There were two first grade girls who lived in Packers Bend. They were Helen and Little Sis, and they were aunt and niece to each other. They were very close and were raised like sisters. There was an accident one day when their Dad and Granddad's automobile ran into the Holy Branch and although he tried to save them, one of them fell into the water and the other tried to save her. They both drowned. We were all so saddened by the accident that from then on, although they fixed the bridge, we were all, including Mr. Brooksie, very leery about crossing it.

Questions About God

I loved to sing in church. By the time I was ten, I was going around singing at all of the neighboring churches. Each church had its own set of "do's and don'ts" but they all taught the same lesson, that if you were bad, the Devil would get you and that God would smite you and punish you too! That really confused me, but it was the only place for me to sing my little heart out. So I listened with one ear open and the other one closed. On one particular Sunday, I was asked to come and sing at a church where the Reverend Little was preaching his fire and brimstone sermon. As I walked through the door, I saw that he was screaming at a fever pitch!

"I tell you God is on the warpath this morning, so alla you sinners beware. He knows who you is, and who you ain't. He knows what you done and who you done it with, and God el git ya! He will smite you dead, you hear me ha! If you don't, amen, heed amen to His word! Amen, so you better git right wid God today."

Then he calmed down and spoke in his natural soft voice and said *"Now we is going to open the doors to the church. But before we do, I hear we have a little gul who wants to bless us with a song."*

The people knew that I could sing, so they started "amening" and" hallaluahing", "yes lawd", and "that child can sing."

I walked up, took my bow, as usual, and started to sing my favorite song.

"Walk with me Lord, walk with me.
Walk with me Lord, walk with me.
While I'm on this tedious journey,
I want you Lord to walk with me."

Oh the church was on fire! The people were just praising and shouting until Rev Little gave the finger to stop.

"Umm mighty fine voice you got there little gul. Oh, you sing the chirping melodies of the Lark, tweet, tweet, and tweet. But it don't mean nothing, I mean nothing, if you ain't been saved. What you say yo name was again?"

"Brenda Marie Eager, Sir"

"Well little Gul, is you saved?"

To which I replied, "I don't know, but I hope so."

"You hope so? You hope so, gul? You *do* want to go to Heaven, don't you?"

"Yes sir."

"Well, you can't go to Heaven unless you been saved and you can't be saved unless you join this here church. This is the house of the Lawd, so come on. I said come on" He glared with his nostrils so wide, that I could see all the way up to the red part inside his nose.

I took one look at Reverend Little, one look at the con-gregation who now was also beckoning me to join, and then the door. I ran out and down the red dirt road as fast as I could until I got tired! I sat down by the side of the road and I sang...

I DON'T BELIEVE

I DON'T BELIEVE IN A GOD LIKE THAT.
I DON'T BELIEVE IN A GOD LIKE THAT.
HE DOESN'T WEAR TWO HATS,
HE CAN'T BE GOOD AND BAD.
I DON'T BELIEVE IN A GOD WHO KILLS THAT

23

COULDN'T BE HIS WILL
WHEN HE MADE US TO LIVE.

HOW CAN YOU SAY YOUR WAYS THE ONLY WAY
AND THAT GOD ONLY LISTENS TO YOU
WELL IF WHAT YOU SAY IS RIGHT
I BEEN WRONG ALL OF MY LIFE
AND THE REST OF MY FAMILY TOO
CAUSE I'VE BEEN TAUGHT THAT GOD IS LOVE
EVERYTHING HE MADE WAS GOOD
FROM EARTH TO HEAVEN ABOVE
AND I THINK THERE'S SOMETHING WRONG WITH
YO FACTS
I DON'T BELIEVE IN A GOD LIKE THAT
NO, NO, NO, NO!
I DON'T BELIEVE IN A GOD LIKE THAT!"

I went straight home to tell Ma'dear. Ma'dear was sitting in her rocker on the porch shelling crowder peas, and noticed my somber face. Then she said,

"Brenda Marie, what's got you in wonderland? Your singing went good today, didn't it?" After filling her in on the day's events, she said,

"What? Why that old scoundrel! He's just mad at yo' Daddy cause your Daddy won't give him one of our cows, baby. He told your Daddy that it was the righteous thing to do and your Daddy told him that the righteous thing for him to do was to grow his own doggone cow. Ha ha! Listen baby, the church is not the building. It is in you!" She sat me down beside her and sang:

YOU CARRY GOD IN YOUR HEART

"BABY, YOU CARRY GOD IN YOUR HEART,
YOU CARRY GOD IN YOUR HEART WHEREVER YOU GO
YOU'RE NEVER APART
HE'S RIGHT THERE WITH YOU WHEREVER YOU ARE.
YOU CARRY GOD, IN YOUR HEART
GOD IS NOT A BUILDING, MADE OF WOOD AND STONE.
IF GOD WAS A BUILDING, CHILD, YOU COULDN'T BRING IT HOME
AND THAT'S TOO HEAVY A BURDEN FOR SUCH A YOUNG CHILD TO OWN
SO LET ME FREE YOUR MIND,
RIGHT HERE AND NOW
YOU CARRY GOD IN YOUR HEART
WHEREVER YOU GO YOUR NEVER APART
HE'S RIGHT THERE WITH YOU WHEREVER YOU ARE
YOU CARRY GOD, IN YOUR HEART"

"Now go on out to that barn and get some sweet potatoes so I can make some pies."

It was truly my Mother's open-mindedness that started me on my Spiritual path.

The Baptism

"LET'S GO DOWN TO THE WATER,
LET'S GO DOWN TO THE WATER,
LET'S GO DOWN TO THE WATER,
TO BE BAPTIZED!"

That song was running through my head like a broken record. The closer it got to Sunday, the more frightened I became. I knew what to expect. I had watched my older cousins get baptized and barely survive. Sunday would be my turn. I had turned twelve years old and in Lower Peachtree, Alabama at the Greater Bells Chapel Baptist church, you were baptized!

Friday night before the big event, I was in bed listening to Ma'dear and Daddy talk about how proud they were that their firstborn was about to be saved. I heard Daddy saying that he, Granddaddy Anderson and Granddaddy's brother, Uncle King, all of whom were Deacons in the church, would be getting up early

26

Sunday morning to go and clean the baptizing pool. He said that they would clear out the big catfish, frogs and snakes but leave the small minnows and tadpoles, because they were too small to hurt anyone. There were also too many of them. Of course, there would be no sleep for me that night.

Sunday morning came too quickly for me. Daddy was already up and out to help clean the pool. Ma'dear was cooking breakfast, which consisted of scrambled eggs, hot biscuits, fried chicken, and homemade sugar cane syrup we made ourselves.

My brothers and sisters, all younger than me, were laughing nervously at me and my upcoming event. But they're laughter was uncomfortable for them, as they contemplated their own future visit to the baptism pool.

Ma'dear got us all dressed and then went to the cabinet to get four white sheets. Oh Lord have mercy! I could just see myself; a young virgin child drowning in a pool of muddy water, while trying to get to Heaven. My heart was starting to beat furiously in my chest. I looked up at Ma'dear and asked if this was all necessary. She said that the Bible said that a person must be baptized to be saved, and to get to Heaven. So I resigned myself to the fact that there was no way out of this Biblical ritual.

The ceremony started at our little wooden church at the bottom of the big red hill that led to my grandparent's house. The church's path was lined by huge magnolias, oak trees and tall pines that Granddaddy sold for lumber. The church was a one-room building built by my father and my uncles. There were about twenty long wooden benches with a big black coal burning heater in the middle of the room.

The graveyard was just outside the window of the church house and I was always afraid that I would see our deceased Native American uncle, Uncle Jeff Dukes, who was buried just outside the door. I was constantly in a state of fear at church. And if that wasn't enough, I looked up to see the Reverend V L Danzy creeping up the aisle. He looked as old as Uncle Jeff, who was 104 when he died. He was bent over at the waist and had steel-grey eyes that met mine as he stopped and gazed at me. I started shaking uncontrollably. He then proceeded to creep up to the pulpit.

After the whole day of preaching and singing, it was finally time. We all walked the short trail to the baptizing pool. The congregation went down the hill to gather themselves around the pool, as if they were gathering around a stage at a concert. Nobody wanted to be in the back, they all coveted their space, just waiting for the main attraction...Me! Ma'dear, Grandma,

28

and Aunt Gooden had stopped with me at the top of the hill. They then commenced to tie two of the sheets to two trees to hide me and then they undressed me and wrapped one sheet around my body and tied strings around my feet to keep my baptismal sheet from exposing my naked body. The sheet was tied at my feet to keep it from rising up in the water. Now I was ready to descend from the mountaintop down into the shaking trembling hands of Reverend Danzy who was going to save me or drown me. I was mortified either way. It took me a while to get down the hill with that rope around my feet. What were they thinking?

I finally got to the pool and they all started singing that doggone song again, "LETS GO DOWN TO THE WATER, TO BE BAPTIZED." As I stood there in fear, I started to try to run the other way. Now I know why the rope was tied around my feet. I kind of fell into the arms of my Daddy who was at the edge of the pool. He then helped me into the pool and the waiting arms of Rev. Danzy. I could feel the mud and the minnows gushing between my toes and I thought to myself, surely I will be toeless by tomorrow.

Reverend Danzy then started muttering some incantation that I could not understand and all of a sudden he flipped me backwards and under the water I went. I was holding my breath as the Sun and the tress and everyone disappeared above me.

29

I was waiting for him to pull me up but he still held me down until I was out of breath. Thank God that the strong arms of my Daddy pulled me up and out of the water. The good Reverend had lost his strength and needed help getting out of the water himself. My, my, my, what a day! I was retching and gasping for air, trying to shake the fish out of my sheet and everybody was jumping and clapping and singing "She's saved! She's saved!"

I was glad to be alive, and I guess that I did make a commitment to God to be the best person I could be. At that age, I did not understand the ritual of it all, but I grew to understand the commitment. That started me on a spiritual journey that I am still traveling today and finding God in all things, in all that I do and in all that I love.

Little House On The Prairie

"Pick that cotton, pull that sack, get off your knees, and bend your back. Pick that cotton, pull that sack. Get off you knees and bend your back!"

Yes, my Daddy was determined to be a farmer. We had ten acres of land that we planted cotton, corn, millet, sugar cane, peanuts, Irish potatoes, sweet potatoes, greens, and all kinds of peas, tomatoes, watermelon, peaches, pears, and others that I can't remember. We also picked the wild blackberries, plums, huckleberries, persimmons, and figs. We had pecans, hickory nuts, and walnuts. We used to store our food in what we called banks. We would bury sweet potatoes and Irish potatoes in the ground and build a bank of straw and dirt over them to keep the frost out because once the frost hit them they would spoil. We cured our meat in the smokehouse. It burned our eyes when we walked in the door, but we would grab the meat as fast as we could and bring it to the kitchen for Ma'dear to cook. And Lord, it was so good.

31

She would fry the meat or smother it down with gravy, and then she would make the best biscuits. We would pour the finest homemade sugar-cane syrup over them and Lord have mercy! That syrup, in its rich dark brown color, would roll off the jar smooth and thick! We had raised our sugar-cane and stripped it pulling off the outer leaves and cutting the crapola out of our little hands. The leaves were as sharp as knives. Afterwards, it was taken to the mill where a horse or mule would pull the sugar around slowly in a hot vat surrounded by a wood and coal burning fire, until it thickened. Then the men would pour each family's syrup from the vat so they could take theirs home. We would be so excited to see how much syrup would be made from our farm. Sometimes we would have as much as twenty to thirty gallons of syrup that would last a year or more. Then, of course, Ma'dear would give it to the neighbors who had not raised sugar-cane that year.

Ma'dear would can all of the vegetables and fruits in mason jars, and store them on shelves in the back room and the kitchen. We had some mighty fine eating growing up!

But I hated pumping water! Our bright red pump was just outside the back door and to prime it, meaning to start the water flow, we would pour just a little water down and then pump real hard and fast until the water came up with every pump of the handle, but our pump did not give big spurts of water like Granddaddy's pump so we had to pump longer and harder to get the water we needed for the house. Once we had enough water for the house, meaning water to cook with, bathe with, and to wash the clothes, we would have to go to the pasture to pump water at another pump for all of the cows, mules, hogs and other farm animals. They drank a lot of water, so Mary, Doe and I would take turns pumping and sometimes the poor cows would be so thirsty they would want to drink all afternoon. They would lick salt from a big yellow salt block that Daddy had bought at the feed store. Sometimes we would have a lick after the cows, whew! Some of the things we tried as kids.

Sometimes I still have nightmares about picking cotton. Pick, pack, pick, and pack. I had a long crocker sack with a home-made strap made from torn up sheets and flour sacks. My goal was to fill it up with cotton four or five times a day and that would insure me of at least a hundred pounds averaging twenty five pounds per sack full.

There was so much more to the farm life which is another whole story in itself. That I just knew that I did not want to grow up and be married to some old pot bellied man who sat around waiting for me to cook three meals a day, winking his eyes at me talking about "Come here Gal!" I knew I wanted to sing!

Just to sing.

I WANT TO SING

I DON'T WANT TO LIVE IN THE COUNTRY
AND I'M TIRED OF PICKING PEAS
I PRAYED SO HARD TO YOU DEAR LORD, TILL
I'M WEARING OUT MY KNEES
I'M TIRED OF GATHERING FIREWOOD, IT
BURNS MUCH TOO FAST.
I DON'T WANT TO CLEAN THE YARD NO
MORE
CAUSE I'M JUST SWEEPING GRASS WITH
GRASS
I WANT TO SING
I WANT TO SING
I'M IN ESTACY
WHEN THERE'S A MELODY, DEEP INSIDE OF
ME
I WANT TO SING.

You Are A Writer

My ninth grade teacher was another one of my favorite teachers. Her name was Rolaneese Bradley, a kind but no nonsense, petite brown-skin lady with short hair and a beautiful smile, when you were lucky enough to see it.

She taught me English and literature. One day she gave us an assignment to write a short story to be turned in to her. I went home and sat up each night for a week and finished my story. I turned it in to her and the next day she called me up to her desk with a stern, almost angry look on her face.

With an accusatory tone, she asked me, "Where did you get this" I shrugged my shoulders, confused not knowing what she meant.

I said, "Ma'am?" And she almost screamed at me and said,

"I said where did you get this? What book did you copy this from?" I then understood.

35

I said "Out of my head. I made it up!" She softened her tone and said,

"You mean you wrote this story yourself?"
"Yes Ma'am." She started to tear up and whispered,

"*You are a great writer!*" It was the first time that someone *else* said those words to me. She said that she wanted to speak with my parents. Later that afternoon, she took me home. She was serious and focused on her mission. No other teachers would ever venture back into Lamberts Quarters for anything. I knew that this was a biggie! She would have to drive for miles through steep hills and winding red dirt roads. The ghostly trees were oak and were filled with moss. The largest of the oaks were loaded with so much moss that they hovered over the road like ghosts. It could be a bit scary. Miss Bradley sat in our one dimensional house and told Ma'dear that I had an exceptional talent for writing poetry and short stories. She was of the opinion that we should publish my story.

Ma'dear said, "Yes I love to read her stories." Of course my momma nor I had the faintest idea what publishing a book meant. So, it would be years before I learned that, but I knew that I loved painting pictures with word and music.

Grandparents: Treasure Beyond Measure!

I had the greatest maternal Grandparents. I had never known my Eager grandparents because they died when my father was a small boy.

Our grandfather, Anderson Clark, used to sit around the wood fire at our house or his house and tell incredibly funny stories about our great, great grandparents and ancestors. We would all laugh until we cried for hours until Ma'dear would say, "Y'all go to bed, now."

Many times she would laugh and join in the storytelling, as well. My grandmother Corine, never thought that Granddaddy was very funny and that itself was hilarious. He would be telling his jokes, adding voices to enhance the flavor of his stories. But grandmother Corine would sometimes look at him with her frowning, shaking head and say,

"You just better not forget my chewing tobacco this week when you go to Thomasville!" Thomasville was the nearest town that had a fully stocked supermarket, not like the makeshift shanties that serviced the local farmers.

And, of course, Granddaddy would forget her tobacco every time. He didn't drink, smoke or dip snuff like a lot of the other farmers, so I think that he would purposely forget to get her little package. On those days, he would be gone all day. My daddy or my Uncle would have to drive because he never learned to drive. My uncle JC tried to teach him to drive a truck once. On the day that my uncle tried to teach Granddaddy to drive, he had barely gotten into the truck when Granddaddy immediately put his foot on the gas. The truck's back tires spun so hard and fast that they left skid marks on the ground. The truck flew backwards and tore down the barn. My uncle calmly told him to get out of the truck and that was the last time he attempted to drive.

My granddaddy was one of the main figures in my life. He was always so kind and caring to me as well as to everyone else. I loved to walk across his land with him and help him feed his cows and hogs. When I was with Granddaddy, it was not work, it was pure joy. I joyously walked at his heels double time, sometimes running to keep up with his brisk pace.

Everybody in Peachtree looked up to my Grandfather. He was the person that all people came to when they needed anything. He would tend to the sick by picking herbs out of the woods, to treat almost anything from burns to whooping cough. When anyone died, they would come and get him, sometimes in the middle of the night. He would help families bury their loved ones. He and Daddy, Granddaddy's brother, Uncle King Clark, Uncle Bemp and JC would all go and dig the graves and then go back home, get dressed and help the families by being the pallbearers. Then Ma'dear, Grandma Corine and Aunt Gooden, Uncle King's wife, would cook the funeral meals for the families. They would have help from other women in the neighborhood, but all of the kids back then loved Ma'dear's and Grandma's cooking.

There were no paved roads in our small town. So once a vehicle turned off the main highway in Upper Peachtree, (there was an upper Peachtree too), they were greeted by the red clay dirt of Alabama which kicked up a whole lot of dust when you drove. A shiny new car would leave Mobile all clean and polished. But, by the time it reached our house, back in the quarters, the car was dusty red and so were the people if they did not roll up the windows! People would come from everywhere doing "Big Meeting" time and my Grandfather would make sure that he killed the fattest cow or hog to feed everyone. Each church in the neighborhood would have a specific day during the summer to have its Big Meeting because the population was so small and everyone wanted to attend everyone else's celebration that honored the church and its members. I would shudder when I had to go to the chicken coop and get chickens for dinner. I had to take them by the head and ring the neck until it broke. Then, I would chop off the head of the chicken with my hatchet and wait for the chicken body to stop jumping before I would have to pick the feathers and clean the chicken, and then cook it. I know it was our way of life, but it's hard to even think about my daily chores, I am such an animal lover.

The women would bake cakes, pies and make potato salad, collard greens and macaroni and cheese, my favorite. They would cook pork roasts, fry chickens, and fry fresh fish. The rock salt was used to make real homemade ice cream. The kids would take turns spinning the handle on the old- fashioned ice cream bucket. They would invite a Minister from another neighborhood to be the speaker for the day and the celebration would last all week until the next Sunday, and then start again at another church. I loved it, because I got to sing at all of them and I ate a lot of macaroni and cheese.

The darn services would last all day with the Ministers squalling at fever pitch. Each one tried to out scream the other. I just sang in-between the sweaty, brow-wiping preachers. Me, Ma'dear, Cousin Gertrude Dukes, Sister Lula Bell Dukes and others carried on with the singing. Grandma Corine would sing until someone noticed her, then she would stop. She was so funny, without even trying to be, most of the time she was dead serious.

Well about four o'clock in the afternoon, when everybody was so hungry that they would have eaten anything, the women lined up outside the church, each one in front of their prized delights that they had been cooking since Saturday morning. Each with a pretty apron tied around their waist and each one waiting for the visiting preacher to have his pick of the food. He would be picking from every spread he saw.

My brothers and sisters and cousins stood in the line and waited until we got to our favorite cooks, which was our Grandmother Corine, Ma'dear and Aunt Gooden. We were picky and there were some boxes we just passed by saying no thank you mam, sure looks good though. We would take our plates and go underneath a tree behind the church and eat 'till we almost passed out. Sometimes, we sat on or near the graves of our departed love ones, which was on the side of the church; although I did not like to do that, but if you really need a seat well...we could not take food into the church so we did the next best thing. Yes Big Meetings were the best.

41

My Grandfather Anderson and Daddy were at odds all the time. Daddy was an ex-Marine who loved to argue and Granddaddy was a quiet, gentle soul who was soft spoken and never raised his voice. I think Daddy was a little angry that Ma'dear insisted that he bring her back to Peachtree after being in Mobile. She really was a Daddy's girl and wanted to be near her parents. Daddy gave in because he wanted to show Granddaddy that he was as good as or a better farmer than him, and frankly no one in Lamberts Quarters were as good a farmer as Granddaddy. He had the biggest hogs, the most cattle, the best corn, the most land, and the best rapport with all the people. Those who sold him his land loved him because when he was younger, he made the best shinny, corn liquor (another word for whiskey). My grandfather was the best business man, but my daddy continued to try. Our farm was only a half a mile from Granddaddy's and once you opened the gate to the left of the house about a hundred yards, you were on Granddaddy's farm. We had ten acres going in the opposite direction. I used to hear Granddaddy trying to tell Daddy how to farm his land to get the best results and Daddy would say, "Now Daddy, ever which kinda way you are professing to educate me on farming, I know already!"

My Granddaddy would say, "Okey Consulia, do it your way." So Daddy did it his way. No matter how hard we worked that farm, it would never compare to Granddaddy's. Bless my Daddy for trying; we probably should have stayed in the city.

Back To The City

When I turned fifteen, my aunt convinced my parents to send me to Mobile to go to school. Of course, I had to come back to the farm every weekend and work, but my friends did not really know.

I was going to be a city girl. I was going to be sophisticated. I would be noticed, because I could sing. I would have lots of friends, and I did, because I could sing. I would have lots of boyfriends, and I did, because I could sing. And I got through high school by the skin of my teeth, because I could sing! I had wonderful friends, Eunice Roland, Glenna Brown, Norma Bernoudy and three crazy play brothers, Enoch Jerome Davis, Willie James Hurst, and my slow talking brother who I like to imitate, Acie Hale. When those three guys and I hung out, I felt like I was one of the guys. I could have been a lot smarter in school. I've since learned that it's great to be popular and smart!

44

A Moment Of Truth

I got the jolt of my life on my sixteenth birthday, my bittersweet sixteenth birthday. My parents gave me a real country surprise party. Daddy picked me up in Mobile and two hours later we were at home and my brothers and sisters, my country cousins and friends were all screaming surprise as we opened the door. There were all kinds of cakes and pies and good food, including homemade ice cream. Ma'dear and Daddy gave me my first birthstone ring, real gold. Then, they took me into the back room and my daddy spoke first.

Daddy said, "Baby I have loved you from the time you were born," Oh no, I know he is not going to tell me that the things I'd been hearing were true.

Ma'dear said, "Brenda Marie, I was pregnant when I met your daddy, he wanted me and he wanted you. We waited 'till we thought you were old enough to share this information with you."

45

I cried, "I am never gonna be old enough for this. Don't tell me that you are not my daddy. I look just like my cousin Linda, I am an Eager!"

And my Daddy, with the most tender, gentle voice and tears in his eyes said to me, "Baby, I am your daddy! When I first saw you, I told my wife, yo momma, that you was mine! I don't care who planted the seed, you are an Eager and I love all my children the same.

I would meet my other Dad years later at a concert that I was performing at, in Atlanta, with Jerry Butler and Earth, Wind and Fire. Our valet knocked on my dressing room door and said "Miss Eager, there is a man out here who says he is your father. I took a long breath, opened the door and there he was, five feet five looking like Jiminy Cricket, my pet name. There was no denying it.

Pops was a funny little man who could tell stories and he and his whole family could sing. And boy could he tell stories. He said to me, "If I had known about you, I would have wanted you, and by the time I found out, your momma and your daddy thought I should wait. And I did." Pops and I shared some wonderful times with his family, and I loved him. But my daddy was Consulia Harris Eager.

First Singing Job

I got my first job right out of high school. Mr. Freddie Lee Harris had a club in Prichard, Alabama right next to Mobile called the Kings Club. I boldly went over to the club one day and asked him for a job singing and he gave it to me. Something was working on my behalf. I went running to my aunt and uncle whom I lived with and told them. They told me that daddy was on his way to take me back to the country in Peachtree.

I pleaded with Daddy and told him that I had a job. He said, "Baby, let me tell you somthin', which ever kind of way it comes out, you getting yourself in some mo mess. Always some money mess singing, Baby."

"But Daddy, I do have a job singing, $40 dollars a night, two nights a week, that's $80 dollars a week. Please Daddy!" Now Daddy was a Taurus and an ex-Marine, who almost always saw things one way, his way!

"Miss! You going home and help your Momma with them children and then you need to get yourself a trade. You can't make no money singing."

Daddy said to me, "Baby pack your stuff and get it in that truck. Yo Momma needs you to help with them children. And that farm."

Now there was Mary, Dorethia, Consulia Jr. CC, Kenneth, and Alvin, so far.

He said that Ma'dear would straighten me out about singing in a club. He said that I could not make money singing and that I should go to a trade school in the fall. I knew I had a chance with Ma'dear, because she always encouraged my music. And I did. She talked to Daddy again and she talked him into letting me go back to Mobile. I started singing at the Kings Club in Prichard, Alabama.

Some Day

I WASN'T BORN IN DETROIT CITY, SO I COULDN'T GO TO SEE THE MOTOWN MAN
AND MEMPHIS TENNESSEE, WAS SO FAR FROM ME
SO I'M SINGING MY SONGS, RIGHT HERE WHERE I AM.

PHILLIDELPHIA, PA IS SO FAR AWAY.
GAMBLE AND HUFF DON'T EVEN KNOW I EXIST.

48

BUT THE FACES I SEE, LOOKING BACK AT ME
MAKES ME KNOW, I WAS MEANT TO DO THIS.
AND SOME DAY YOURE GONNA SEE ME
SOMEDAY YOUR GONNA KNOW MY NAME
IMPOSSIBLE IT MAY SEEM, BUT I BELIEVE IN
THIS DREAM AND NO ONE CAN'T NOBODY,
NOBODY TAKE IT AWAY, AWAY AWAY.

WELL I CAN SEE A CHANGE A COMIN',
SOMEDAY I'LL TAKE THAT TICKET TO RIDE,
I'LL CATCH A PLANE, A BUS, A ROLLING
LOCOMOTIVE, GONNA CHASE THAT DREAM
OF MINE

AND SOMEDAY YOUR GONNA SEE ME.

Growing Up The Hard Way or One Dress And A Dream

I met my future husband at that same club two years later, but first I had taken a short trip to New York to seek my fame and fortune.

My cousin had driven his new long shinny Cadillac from New York for a visit. By the time he pulled up in our yard, the car was covered with the red clay dust of Alabama. He got out shaking the dust from his clothes and sat and talked. He told Ma'dear and Daddy that I should come back to New York with him and his wife and that there were plenty of clubs that I could sing in and get discovered. Well, daddy of course said no, and then Ma'dear said, "Well, God lives in New York too!" I packed my few rags and waited until my cousin returned later that evening. I was shocked when he showed up with his girlfriend and eight other people in the car. I had a lot of cousins who wanted to pursue their dreams as well. I rode all the way from Peachtree Alabama to New York City lying across five grown people in the back seat of that infamous Cadillac. I was determined to get there!

I went to the famous Apollo Theater to audition and was turned away at the door. I wound up getting a job in the Manhattan garment district, putting sequins and stones on cloths that were being made into the most beautiful gowns that I had only dreamed of wearing. That lasted six months and I couldn't even catch a fire, so I tucked my tail home and went back to Mobile.

Meeting Mr. Lee

I went to my cousin, Poochie's house, when I got back to Mobile. She was only a couple of years older than me and was married with a beautiful home. I lied and told her that I was doing good and that I was just home for a visit. I was too embarrassed to tell her the truth.

Poochie suggested that we go out to my old spot The Kings Club, so we did. We were having some fun dancing when she looked up and said "Oh Lawd, here comes that old black ass Mack Donald Lee. What ever you do, do not talk to him! He is a player, been married, fixing to be married again. Got one kid and one on the way."

Don sashayed over towards me, and I felt weak. It seemed like he was walking on air, he was so smooth. He was dark and handsome. I thought he looked like Sidney Pointier

He said to me "Hay, what's your name, have I seen you here before?"

And my cousin Poochie said to him, "No you have not, and you probably won't see her again, my cousin is a singer and making something of herself, so take your black ass on away from here with your bull."

Ignoring Poochie, Don said to me, "Do you talk or do you just sing."

I said "Ah, um I talk."

The band asked me to sing a couple of songs, so I sang "DO RIGHT WOMAN", Aretha's new song. And *OPEN THE DOOR TO YOUR HEART,* a popular number that was one of my favorites.

Poochie had her mouth stuck out the rest of the night. When Don asked if he could take me home, she answered "Hell no! She came with me and she is leaving with me!"

Well, Mack Donald Lee took me home that night and every other night after that. We moved to Chicago, and seven months later, I was pregnant. We went to the courthouse in downtown Chicago, and got married on his lunch hour. He went back to work and I went back to Mobile to have a baby. I trusted my Ma'dear to take care of me.

My beautiful Grandma Corine and my Grand-daddy Anderson Clark helped Ma'dear out. Ma'dear just having had her tenth child, my brother John, was still mending. Grandma Corine would bake my favorite white-icing cake, three layers with homemade frosting. It was good! She would walk all the way from their house down the road to ours. I could see her stop and rest along the way but she was determined to bring that cake to me. Oh, how I miss them!

Well, I had been home in Lower Peachtree with my family for two months now and I was about to experience some major changes in my young life again.

4-4-68

D o you remember where you were? April 4th 1968, I was at my mother's house in Lower Peachtree, and was having the worst nightmare of my life. I dreamed that I was in a country church and there was a funeral. I was feeling such grief that I could hardly breathe. I could see the casket as I entered the church. It was deep purple, with red velvet drapes around the back of it. I was afraid to see who was in the casket because I knew that it would be a loved one, I just didn't know which one. Just as I got close enough to see who it was, I screamed and sat straight up in the bed. A pain came out of no where and landed in my lower back. Ma'dear came running and put her hand on my back and pressed upward. I was amazed then the pain just disappeared."

"How did you do that, Superwoman!" she said, "It will be back child, you in labor." Now! I was scared!

Ma'dear, who never learned to drive, called Ms. Tooter Kimbrough to drive me to the hospital which was fifty miles away. We stopped by my grandparents house who were arguing over who was going to go to the hospital with me. My grandmother said, "I am the woman, so I am going!" My grandfather said, "Corine, I have the money, so I am going!" And he did.

My water broke an hour after I got to the hospital.

Nine hours later, the sadistic nurse was still telling me not to push, because they were waiting for my doctor. He was on a fishing trip.

Finally a little colored maid in a grey dress, with a pink collar, came in to the room pretending to be cleaning, and cautiously said to me, "Baby, you wanna live and you want yo baby to live, you best to start pushing, I don't care what dey say!"

And so I pushed Michelle out late that afternoon and was stitched up and taken to my room. I was heavily sedated and went to sleep. I awoke to see my Grandfather, who reminds me of a brown smiling Buddha, gazing out of the window with tears streaming down his face. Ma'dear was crying too.

I panicked! "What's wrong, is my baby alright,"

Ma'dear said, "Ssssh! The baby is fine." Then biting her bottom lip as she always did when she was mad or upset, she said. "They just killed Dr. King."

I was drifting off again and woke up later. My precious Grandfather was still sitting at the window crying silent tears. His coveralls were now wet beneath his chin. I had never seen some one with that much pain in his face.

I began telling Ma'dear, "I dreamed you told me that Dr Martin Luther King had been killed." Ma'dear just took me in her arms, looked at me, her own tears flowing, and I knew that it was not a dream. It was Dr. King in the dream!

WE SHALL OVER COME, WE SHALL OVER-COME SOMEDAY.

I was too young to process the agony, and the anger that I was feeling, and yet, hold on to the joy of giving birth to one of the greatest women I know, Michelle, Mon belle.

One year later I was to join the movement.

The Windy City, Again

Michelle was six months old when I returned to Chicago and to Don. He kept putting off our return date month after month until I called him and told him that if he did not send for us, he could just forget it! I had gotten hold of a magazine from Chicago that was popular at the time. It printed love stories for Blacks that showcased stories with Black models. I picked up one particular magazine and who did I see all hugged up with another beautiful female model in a husband and wife embrace...Don!

Oh, I lost my mind. Here I was in Mobile at his Mother's house, taking care of Michelle while he was in Chicago posing with some cutie model doing love scenes, and all the while telling me that he was looking for work and that as soon as he could afford to, he would send for us. It was mighty funny how he found the money when I got fighting mad!

Don's mother was a Cooter. She was mean! I don't think that she liked anybody, especially me.

I was staying at her house with Don's Dad, Mr. Lee who was a kind soul. He never raised his voice and always tried to stay out of his wife's way. If she wasn't fussing, she was walking around talking to herself.

She would say to me, "Girl, I don't know who you think you are and where Don got you from, but I will be glad when he takes you away from here." She never wanted to hold Michelle either and I was busting my butt to please her; cleaning behind myself and my newborn child, cleaning the floors, the dishes, and doing whatever I could do to put a smile on her face. It was all a wasted effort. One day she went out of town for a week and gave me strict orders that everything had better be the same way she left it when she returned. Mr. Lee did not go. But, during that time, we had a few nice talks and he kind of apologized for some of the things that she had said. He told me that she did not mean most of what she said, but I was sure to keep everything the way she wanted it. She had bought a new pan that was so cheap it hardly had any weight to it at all. It was a round tin pan used for washing dishes. I pulled it out of the cupboard and although my mind told me not to, I needed something to wash the dishes in and there was nothing else. My logic deduced that that was why she bought it. I filled it halfway with water and sat it on the stove to heat up, in order to wash the dishes. My father-in-law had cooked a great meal, mustard greens, chicken, rice and cornbread. I washed the dishes and started to pour the water out of the pan when I saw the pan had a ring around it where the water had been heated. Panic struck! I scraped and washed that pan, trying my best to make that ring disappear. I put it out in the sun hoping that it would all become one color again. Nope, that did not happen. I was beside myself with worry. I wished that I had had the money to go and get another one, but I did not. So I waited the three days for her to come home.

When she got to the house, she barely spoke as she went through the house examining things, counting silverware, sniffing her clothes. She was a small woman with small piercing eyes that looked right through your soul and had no warmth at all. I am sure that she was not always that way and something must have hurt her somewhere in her life to lead to her mistrustful nature. Later that evening, she went to the kitchen to cook, and I heard her yell, "Girl, what did you do to my pan?"

I started to try to explain that the heat made the ring, and as I was holding Michelle in my arms she took a swing at me and almost knocked me down with the baby. That was enough! I called my sister Mary and she was over to that house in a half hour and I packed up my clothes and went to her house and stayed until Mr. Mack Donald Lee finally sent for us. I never told Don how his Mother had treated us. I figured that I was not going to stay with her ever again, and I didn't.

Don had several brothers and sisters. My favorite two were Minnie and Howard. They had one brother that left home when he got grown and never came back, not even when people died, never...I wonder why.

Don had set up house on the south side of Chicago in Lake Meadows. It was a beautiful two-bedroom apartment, completely furnished. Besides his modeling job, he worked at Goldblatts furniture store, close enough to walk to work.

I did not like the furniture, olive green French provincial old folks furniture that they wrap plastic around, but it was home and he had it all fixed up for us. On the coffee table was the biggest ash tray that I had ever seen. It was a glass in the shape of a leaf; it was so heavy that I did not like to pick it up. The bedrooms were nicer, with new bedding. Wow! I had never had such beautiful bedspreads and blankets before, so I was some happy, did not fuss, did not even think about the last six months. I was home with my husband and we were a family!

I soon took a job, at Don's request. I started working at Lake Shore National bank downtown Chicago. I would get up, take Michelle to the baby

61

sitter then take the train to downtown till four o'clock, get the train back, pick up Michelle, come home and cook and have it ready by the time Don got home at seven.

This was routine for about six months. Don started coming home later and later on Fridays, until it became Saturday morning when he'd come in. Me, I had been sitting in the window all night worried, 'till I see him walking up the street without a care in the world. He would sashay into the room and ask for breakfast as if he had been home all night. My worry would turn to anger, but he would warn me not to make a fuss, that he was sleepy and was gonna go to bed. One such morning, he came in late, after he told me to reheat the food, said he had the munches, and I didn't even know what the munchies were. I was mumbling under my breath about why he stayed out 'till morning knowing that he would wanna fight, and again he told me to fix my face.

Well, I had had enough. I was so mad, Michelle was asleep, so I went into the living room, picked up that heavy leaf ashtray, walked into the bedroom, held it over his head, and then he opened his left eye, and started to laugh. "Girl,, you trying to hit me with that ashtray? I can't trust you enough to go to sleep with you inside, so I think I will put your ass out." We wrestled as he started to drag me. I tried to hold on to the bed post, the TV, the sofa, but he kept dragging me, my gown came off and now I was totally naked when he closed the door. I was knocking softly begging him to let me back in, but he did not. I went to my best friend Jo Marie's house next door and she and her husband, Leonard, took me in and gave me some clothes.

Don and I were not happy much together after that. He got more and more angry and took that anger out on me. Looking back, I now can see that he most likely had someone else...duh.

I am glad though that that beautiful man graced my life. With all of his frustrations and anger, he still helped to bring my beautiful daughter and grandchildren to me. We had shared some beautiful moments together and voiced some regrets and apologies to one another and up until his death; we remained friends and shared our children. Don came to LA to give Michelle to Paul, our son-in-law, at their wedding and the boys Corey and Quinton got to know their Grandpa Don, so I can only be grateful!

The Movement

I was still determined to sing somewhere. One Wednesday night, I went to the Parkway Ballroom on the south side of Chicago where Operation Breadbasket choir rehearsed and there I met Pat Henley one of the soloist. I told her that I was a singer and that I wanted to join the choir. She then took me to the young, electrifying, handsome preacher Jesse Jackson who I had been hearing on the radio. He asked me one question, "Can you sing?" and I said, "Yes!"

He said, "Good, you singing Saturday morning", and that was that. I was now one of four soloists from the choir who sang and traveled with Rev. Jesse Louis Jackson and the Ben Branch Orchestra, headed by Dr. King's favorite musician Ben Branch. Dr. King had named Ben the Pied Piper of the movement and Jesse Rev. Jesse Louis Jackson named us "The Pipperettes of Freedom". We hated the name, but Pat Henley, Lois Scott, Sue Conway and myself would lock arm in arm and sing the freedom songs of the times and the hopes and aspirations for the future.

The Capitol Theater would come alive on Saturday mornings; Rev. Jesse Louis Jackson would open up with the chant:

"I AM SOMEBODY!
I AM SOMEBODY!
I MAY BE BLACK, BUT I AM SOMEBODY!
I MAY BE POOR, BUT I AM SOMEBODY!
I MAY BE DISINFRANCHISED, BUT I AM SOME-BODY!
I MUST BE RESPECTED, I MUST BE PROTECTED! I AM SOME BODY.
I AM GOD'S CHILD!"

We believed it, we embodied it, and we wanted to make a difference. At the meetings, it was common to see people like Harry Belafonte, Bill Cosby, Quincy Jones, Nancy Wilson, and Sammy Davis. My friend Dick Gregory before the fast, and Jean Seberg were there as regulars. These people risked their careers to take a stand for justice and equality. I remember us taking Jean Seberg, Miss Joan of Arc herself, to the Queen of the Sea Soul Food restaurant, where she had a great time eating collard greens, smothered chicken, black eyed peas and candied yams. She loved it, too! She ate every pea on her plate! I was there when

Cannonball Adderly recorded country preacher right at the meeting.

Les McCann and Eddie Harris would also come and play, and many more. Mickey Stevenson would come and bring Kim Weston to sing Lift Every Voice and Sing, like I had never heard it before, with so much soul and passion.

Then there were our dear Fred Hampton and Mark Clark of the Chicago Panther party. I remember when the Chicago police and Mr. Hanrahan broke in and slaughtered Fred and Mark in what was called the "Predawn Raid." It was discovered that over two hundred bullets had been fired into his place.

The Pipperettes and I walked the picket lines. We sang at rallies across the country. I was there singing when Carl Stokes was elected to his second term in Cleveland, Ohio. I was there singing when Perren Mitchell was elected in Baltimore, Maryland. I was there singing when Walter Fauntleroy was elected in Washington, DC. I was there singing when Mayor Richard Hatcher was elected in Indianapolis, Indiana. I was there singing when Kenneth Gibson was elected in New Jersey. We sang, we marched, sometimes in the rain and sometimes in the snow! We sang on top of buses, before and after Jesse's speeches. We sang on flat bed trucks in the rain. We went door to door to get people to vote. We did everything we could do to get the people to come out, vote and be a part of the necessary change!

First Recording Contract

J esse got us our first record contract with the great Sax records in Memphis, Tennessee. We were so excited to be signed by the great Al Bell himself, who had artists like The Staple singers, Sam and Dave, Isaac Hayes, Johnnie Taylor, my friends The Emotions, The Barkays, and many more. Al walked into the room with a record in his hand, plunked it down on the table and said, "Young ladies, what I have here is your first hit record! Nobody else has even heard it. I know it's a hit and if you trust me, you will be on the top of the charts with this one." Oh, we were so excited!

We listened...I spoke up.

"I can't hear it." Al's smile turned up side down and he said "listen again" we listened and again I said, "Nope, can't hear it, don't like it."

By now he is irritated, and spoke with a hint of an ultimatum. We were foolish enough to say no again and he picked up the record and left the meeting. The song...

"WHEN YOU'RE WEARY, FEELING SMALL, WHEN TEARS ARE IN YOUR EYES I WILL DRY THEM ALL. Yes that song was Simon and Garfunkel's Bridge over troubled waters which became one of the greatest and most reorded songs in music history.

Well Mr. Al Bell took his song and left to go back to Memphis. We wound up singing backups for Roberta Flack and my friend Donny Hathaway. I loved singing with Donny. He was very dear to me. I love my Brother to this day. One evening I went to Donny's house to rehearse along with the Piperettes. I got there before the rest of them and Donny and I had some time to just kick it and talk. He sat at the piano gulping honey right out of the bottle. He then said to me,"Hey Brenda, I got a song here that I am thinking of recording, I want to play it for you and you tell me honestly if you think it's a hit." I said, "Sure", as he strapped on his new piano across his shoulder, which was something new too. He started to play the intro to "This Christmas". I jumped up and danced the whole song. He told me that my friend Nadine McKinnor had written the lyrics and I said that it was a hit and Lord knows it was and is today! Wish I had helped to write it.

A year later Jesse reluctantly let me out of my contract to go and record with the great Jerry Butler. I had co-written a song with Jesse's baby brother Chuck, who took the demo to Jerry and he liked the song and the singer. We became a duet and as they say, the rest is history...

The years with Jerry were a great learning experience for me. I was a little country girl from Alabama with hit records, but as Jerry put it, not much experience, and as they say in the business, I had not paid my dues. I thought that picking a hundred pounds of cotton, and all the other chores on the farm was paying dues, but it wasn't! That was just growing up. I would pay though in the years to come.

Landed In Heaven

The Apollo Theater, Wow, Just five years ago, I had tried to audition here and was turned away at the door, now the marquis outside said, "Appearing tonight! JERRY BUTLER AND BRENDA LEE EAGER!" It was cold and raining that night, but I did not care. We had a hit record "AINT UNDERSTANDING MELLO", and I was gonna sing at the famous Apollo theater in New York City. I only wished Ma'dear, Daddy, Mary, Dorethia, Consulia Jr, CC, Kenneth, Debra Ann, Alvin, Timothy, John, and Baby Willie could see their oldest sister, and see how the whole theater rose to their feet when I walked onto the stage. I had not even opened my mouth and they were screaming! Jerry whispered in my ear, "Stand there a moment and let them love you", and I did! What a feeling!

We knew we had something special with "AINT UNDER-STANDING MELLO". It was a magical performance. Jerry and I walked into the studio, the track started to play, we looked at each other and sang the whole song down and that was that. We stood flat footed, sang that song and that is the way you heard it. Thanks to you, it is still one of the all time great soul classics that is still being played. Today.

Jerry and I came to Los Angeles one winter to do Soul Train. The show featured Jerry and me and Ike and Tina Turner. We left Chicago in a blizzard and landed where palm trees were swinging in the warm breeze and Keg Johnson, our driver, greeted us in Bermuda shorts. I knew that I had landed in heaven and it would be where I would live.

Song Writing

I love to write! I started writing in the third grade. I was different, you think? My teacher called me Granny, because I would be writing on pieces of paper or talking to myself during recess while the other kids were outside playing. I liked being by myself. I had enough brothers and sisters, to play with. I valued my alone time. Sometimes I would sneak off to my Granddaddy's pasture, lean my back against my favorite oak tree and venture deep into my own imagination to find characters and colors to bring my poems and short stories to life. We had no television at that time, so I read a lot and still today, I have a very vivid imagination! I can create a story or a song starting out with a blank sheet of paper. That is my canvas on which to paint something beautiful!

We did have a radio that played rhythm and blues late at night and Gospel on Sunday mornings. Oh, how I loved the Gospel! My first love was Mahalia Jackson. She would wrap her Soul around a song and use her whole body to express it. What a voice! It was as strong as a mountain, yet would caress you like a mother with her child. I learned a lot from Miss Mahalia. I would meet her years later in Chicago at Operation Breadbasket. She was in a wheelchair at that time. We got to have a wonderful conversation.

Then, I heard Albertina Walker and the Caravans, live. There was Albertina, Shirley Caesar, Josephine Howard, Inez Andrews, and Casetta George, Dorothy Norwood and later Delores Washington. I was spellbound when I heard them sing. Such strong and passionate harmonies! I tried to look like Albertina, whose picture I had seen on an album cover my cousin had. They are still my favorite Gospel group today. Oh, and I love the great Edna Galmon Cooke, and The Barrett Sisters of Chicago.

On Sunday mornings, I could hear the Great Quartet singers also. I loved The Soul Stirrers with the great Sam Cook. The Mighty Clouds of Joy, The Hi Way QCs, The Swan Silverstones, The Dixie Hummingbirds, The Five Blind Boys of Alabama and many more. I was getting a real education in Gospel singing. It filled my soul with joy!

Somebody's Somebody

After I had moved from Chicago to Los Angeles, I found that work was harder to come by. My boyfriend at the time, Bob and I drove out to California with my five-year-old daughter, Michelle, and two cats. Things were good for awhile. Money got funny after about three years, but we continued writing all the time. Bob is still my dear friend to this day. Although we did not stay together, we started to have different dreams. He started saying I was too old to make it in the business. I never knew that! And that was twenty five years ago! Lord, what would he say now!

Now when I write a song, it comes in a matter of minutes, it just flows through me. I know its good. One came in about twenty minutes. Mavis Staples of the famous Staple singers had let her producer at the time listen to some of my songs and she called me one day whispering.

"Uh Brent, this is Mavis, uh Print is in his office and he is reading your lyrics girl. He said for me to call you and tell you to send him some more lyrics, just the lyrics, he don't want the music." He said, "Mavis, that Brenda Lee Eager is one of the best writers I have seen in a while! So Brent get them lyrics off right away. He wants to put his music to your lyrics."

I sent Prince the lyrics that I had written in twenty minutes. He wrote the music, produced it, and it became a double platinum record. What a thrill for all of us!

I had actually written the song for Eddie Kendricks and David Ruffin of the Temptations who had asked me to do so because they wanted to do a duet. Our mutual friend, Charles Davis had us all on a three way telephone call and I told them that I would have a song in a couple of days. When I woke up with the song. My friend, Hilliard put a track together and we sang a demo and sent it to Eddie. This was prior to me sending it to Mavis. But the guys never got a chance to record it. They both passed away and then our mutual friend Charles Davies passed away too. But the song lives on today! "IT'S TWO O'CLOCK IN THE MORNING, AND I JUST CAN'T SLEEP." *It was two o'clock in the morning and I could not sleep.* "OUTSIDE THE RAIN IS POURING, I'M LONE-SOME AS CAN BE." *Yep, it was raining and I was as lonesome.*

"MAYBE TONIGHT WILL BE DIFFERENT, THAN THE NIGHTS BEFORE

I NEED TO HAVE SOMEONE BESIDE ME,
DON'T WANNA BE ALONE NO MORE
TONIGHT I WANNA BE SOMEBODY'S, SOME-
BODY".

Collaborating is sacred to me. I need to feel a positive connection with the other writer. It's kind of like a communion of souls who give birth to music that marries lyrics and melodies. Billy Osborne of LTD fame and I have written a lot of songs over the last twenty years. I love to write with Billy. We laugh, we slap hands, we get mad, and we would fuss. He'd cuss, verbally fight, and then make up by writing another song. His lady was always so loving and patient with us, when we worked together.

Aretha Episode

After about ten years of us hashing out songs, Bobby Womack called me one day and said, "Hey Bren, this is Bobby. Retha is looking for songs. You and Billy should send her some of yours. Bobby and Shirley Brown, "Woman to Woman"fame, had already recorded one of our songs. Billy and I sent Aretha six songs, some written just for her.

About six weeks later the phone rang. I was in the shower, singing of course.

I jumped out of the shower with just a towel wrapped around me as I answered the phone.

"Hello. Hello Brenda this is Aretha".

And I said, "Aretha who?"

Laughing, she said, "Brenda this is Aretha Franklin. How is Jerry?"

78

I knew it was her by then, so I said, "Woman, I have been waiting for twenty years for you to call me!"

She laughed again and said "I got your songs and I love all of them. As a matter of fact, I want to record all of them. Now can I have these songs, because I don't want you to give them to any one else. I don't like the project that I am doing and I am going to start over with your songs. Clive Davis will be calling you next."

As I hung up the phone, I screamed, jumped around waved my hands in praise, as my towel fell to the floor.

I immediately called Billy and told him to get over to my house right away. I told him that Aretha had called and wanted all of the songs we had sent her. I repeated what Aretha had told me that Clive Davis would be calling next. Billy rushed from the valley to the Wilshire area, walked into my house we both fell on our knees thanking God and crying like babies. We gained our composure and waited for Clive to call. We would look at each other and then the phone. He was supposed to call around four thirty. We waited until about seven. Billy went home. I continued staring at the phone trying to make it ring. But Clive never called and we would not hear from Aretha for another ten years.

Compelled Passion

But when you're a singer/songwriter, you can't stop. A song will wake you up in the middle of the night. It will creep into your dreams and get you up at three in the morning. I kept a pad or piece of paper by the bed so I could just reach over and scribble it down while I tried not to wake up. Don't think that you're going to remember it in the morning, you won't! The universe is funny, it will give you what you ask for, but you've got to take it when it is being given.

The first time I heard, "LIKE A SNOWBALL ROLLING DOWN THE SIDE OF A SNOW COVERED HILL, ITS GROWING, LIKE THE SIZE OF THE FISH THAT THE MAN CLAIMED BROKE HIS REEL, ITS GROWING. Blew my mind! I wanted to paint pictures like my friend Smokey Robinson. I wanted to create beautiful melodies, with colors, contrast and passion with deep emotion. These are the tools that I got from the masters. From Yip Harburg with SOME WHERE OVER THE RAINBOW to Bobby Womack with IF

YOU THINK YOUR LONELY NOW to the social content of my brother Curtis Mayfield' PEOPLE GET READY. Irving Berlin, Rogers and Hammerstein, Alan and Marylin Bergman, PEOPLE, PEOPLE WHO NEED PEOPLE. Burt Bacharach and Hal David, to Marvin's WHAT'S GOIN ON and Sam's, CHANGE IS GONNA COME, and so many more. I studied only the hits, the top ten in billboard. Bob, my ex, was a good guy, but stubborn, yet tenacious, also a great musician, and if I had any notion of quitting when times were tough back then, he would say, "Bone up! Are you gonna sit there and cry cause your fingers are bleeding from cleaning apartments or you gonna bandage your fingers dry your eyes and write a song?" I bandaged my fingers dried my eyes and spent most of the night writing a song. That was a long time ago and I am still compelled to write a song!

Some Of My Teachers

When I heard Jazz and rhythm and blues, it really broadened my horizons as a singer. My Ma'dear would let me come out of the cotton field every time Sarah Vaughn was on the radio. She would yell out "Brenda Marie, Miss Sarah Vaughn, your favorite singer is on the radio right now!" I would come a running to hear Sarah sing "BROKEN HEARTED MELODY. Wow, what phrasing and color. I called her my liquid singer, because she was flowing smooth like warm butter. She could move in and out of octaves without effort and carry you along the magical melodies of the song's Yeah, Sassy smooth. I wanted to sing that music like Miss Sarah.

STARTING OVER

I'M STARING OUT INTO A NEW BE-GINNING
LOOKING IN YOUR EYES IT'S OH SO CLEAR
THE PAIN WE'VE CAUSED EACH OTHER ALL IS ENDING
WERE STARTING OVER BABY RIGHT NOW

RIGHT HERE
A VISION OF A NEW DAY
THE CHANGING OF OUR MINDS
THE LOVE WE BOTH DISCOVERED
WE ALMOST LEFT BEHIND
YOU'RE LOOKING BETTER THAN I'VE EVER
SEEN YOU
I REALLY LIKE THE WAY YOU WEAR YOUR
HAIR
I'M UNDERSTANDING ALL MISUNDERSTAND-
INGS
DO ANYTHING I CAN TO SHARE I CARE
LETS EMBRACE THIS NEW BEGINNING
SO WARM AND WONDERFUL
THE SWEETEST REVIVAL
STARTING OVER.

SOME PEOPLE NEVER TAKE THE TIME TO
START AGAIN
RESENTMENT ANGER PRIDE,
KEEPS THEM FROM BEING FRIENDS
BUT IT FREES THE SOUL WHEN YOU MAKE
AMMENDS
THEN YOU CAN START AGAIN

NOW MY DAYS ARE FILLED WITH LAUGHTER
AND MY NIGHTS ARE FILLED WITH BLISS
AND WHEN WE GET DISTRACTED FROM THE
WISDOM

WE BRING EACH OTHER BACK WITH JUST
ONE KISS
WEVE HAD A REVELATION
AND NOW WE SEE THE LIGHT
SO GOOD TOGTHER BABY, WE FINALLY GOT
IT RIGHT
SO GOOD TOGETHER BABY,
LET'S KEEP ON STARTING OVER

And Lady D., Miss Dinah Washington, has been
described as kind of rough, with a mouth like a sailor.
She did not like a lot of people, but I loved her. She
laid into a song, made love to it with strength and
vulnerability. She, like Sarah, knew how to paint
those pictures.

MORE THAN BEAUTIFUL

PRETTIER THAN THE REDDEST ROSE OF
SPRING
AS IT KISSES THE MORNING DEW
MY DARLING YOU'RE
SO MUCH LOVELIER THAN A SUMMER SUN
WHEN THE EVENING COMES
AS IT DANCES OUT OF VIEW
BRIGHTER, THAN HEAVEN'S BRIGHTEST STAR
LIGHTING UP THE DARKEST NIGHT
YOU LIGHT MY WORLD WITH YOUR SMILE
LIFE WITHOUT YOU WOULDN'T BE WORTH-
WHILE

I WANT YOU TO KNOW
THAT I LOVE YOU SO

AND STILL I CANT BELIEVE
SOMEONE SO BEAUTIFUL LOVING ME
A FACE LIKE AND ANGEL
A HEART OF GOLD
A RADIENT SOUL
SENT FROM UP ABOVE
JUST FOR ME TO LOVE

YOU ARE
MORE THAN BEAUTIFUL
MORE THAN ELOQUENT
MORE THAN BEAUTIFUL
I KNOW YOU ARE HEAVEN SENT.

Some of you may not know this, but I became a Staple singer for a hot minute. Mavis was leaving, and pops asked me to join the group.

"Eerr eerr Brenda, Mavis is leaving the group and we need somebody to carry on that vibration." We rehearsed three months and just as I was about to put on my Staple singers outfit, Mavis came back and said, get back Montana! I changed my mind! Awe Awe umm.

Mavis recorded this Eager/Osborne song a couple of years ago.

85

I STILL BELIEVE

"I STILL BELIEVE IN YOU"
WHEN OUTSIDE PRESSURES KNOCK YOU TO
YOUR KNEES
COME REST IN MY ARMS, I'LL GIVE YOU
RELIEF
WHEN THEY TRY TO DESTROY YOUR
CONFIDENCE
DON'T GIVE THEM THE SATISFACTION,
NOT AT YOUR EXPENSE
CAUSE YOU'VE GOT A FRIEND
WHO'LL SEE YOU THROUGH
THE WHOLE WORLD CAN TURN ITS BACK
BUT
I STILL BELIEVE IN YOU

I STILL BELIEVE IN YA
I STILL BELIEVE
I STILL BELIEVE IN YA
I STILL BELIEVE

NOTHIN' CAN SHAKE MY FAITH IN YOU

THOUGH MANY TRIED, THEY COULD NOT
BREAK THROUGH
MY CONVICTION IS STRONG, MY LOVE IS
STR-ONGER STILL

I KNOW WITHOUT A DOUBT, YOU CAN GET
OVER ANY HILL

I WILL ENCOURAGE YOU
IN EVERTHING YOU DO
EVEN WHEN YOU DOUBT YOURSELF
I STILL BELIEVE IN YOU!

I'VE WATCHED YOU STUMBLE BUT NEVER
FALL
SEEN YOU TIME AND TIME AGAIN, YOUR
BACK AGAINST THE WALL!

I'VE FELT THE PAIN YOU SOMETIMES HAD
TO SUFFER THROUGH
BUT LIKE A TREE
I WILL NO T BE MOVED
I STILL BELIEVE IN YOU,
 MY BROTHER
MY FATHER
MY TEACHER
MY PREACHER
MY SON
MY DAUGHER
ITS SOLID AS A ROCK, MY LOVE, IS SOLID AS
A ROCK, I BELIEVE IN YOU

Aretha, what can I say, the greatest. Perfect phrasing, placement and downright soul of the ages. This is one of the songs I sent to her.

JUST TO BE LOVED

IVE BEEN THROUGHT THE FIRE
AND I'VE WEATHERED THE STORM
THROUGH IT ALL, YOUR LOVE HAS KEPT ME
SAFE FROM HURT AND HARM.
YEA THE FIRES RAGED, AND SOMETIMES
THE RAINS CAME DOWN
BUT YO-U WERE THERE TO SHELTER ME
OH, WHAT A LOVE I'VE FOUND

SOME WHERE IN MY LIFETIME, I MUST HAVE
DONE SOMETHING GOOD FOR SOMEBODY
HOW ELSE IN THE WORLD
COULD I DESERVE SOMEONE LIKE YOU
SOME ONE WHO GIVES HIS LOVE SO
COMPLETELY
SO SWEETLY
ASKING ONLY FOR MY LOVE IN RETURN,
THAT I GIVE SO WILLINGLY
EVERY PART OF ME

I WOULD GIVE AWAY MY EARTHLY THINGS
MANSIONS, MONEY, DIAMOND RINGS

I WOULD GIVE MY ALL IN ALL I DO
JUST TO BE LOVED BY YOU

GOD SURELY HAS SMILED ON ME
YOU WERE THE ANSWER TO ALL MY PRAYERS
I'VE WAITED MY WHOLE LIFE FOR YOU
BABY, BUT YOU CAME RIGHT ON TIME
YOU THRILL ME, YOU FILL ME
WITH A LOVE SO ALL ENCOMPASSING
AND ALL THAT I HAVE JUST CAN'T COMPARE
TO THE JOY THAT YOU BRING
AND THE LOVE THAT WE SHARE.

THE GREATEST GIFT, ANYONE CAN GIVE
IS LOVE FROM THE HEART
CAUSE TO LOVE AND BE LOVED
IS TO TRULY LIVE

Now Gladys Knight is my feisty sister. I enjoyed every minute I spent with Gladys. Here is one of my favorite songs that Osborne and I actually wrote with Gladys in mind.

If you have real friends in this world, you've got a treasure beyond measure, and never take them for granted. And this is what I had in mind when I wrote:

FRIENDS

HERE WE ARE ONCE AGAIN
YOU AND ME, MY OLD FRIEND
YES IT'S BEEN AWHILE,
AND I SURE COULD USE YOUR SMILE
MIGHT I SAY I'VE MISSED YOU, TOO.
THERES SOME CHANGES I BEEN GOING
THROUGH
YOU COULD'NT HAVE COME AT A BETTER
TIME
OH, YOU MUST HAVE READ MY MIND

YOU'VE BEEN THERE FROM THE BE-GINNING
YOU KNOW ME BETTER THAN ANYONE
YOU KNOW WHERE I WANNA GO
CAUSE YOU KNOW WHERE I'M COMING FROM

YOU'VE SEEN ME AT MY WEAKEST,
WHEN SOMETIMES I HAD TO COM-PROMISE
AND YOU'VE NEVER QUESTIONED MY LIFES-
TYLE,
YOU NEVER CRITICISE.
AND FRIENDS LIKE YOU AND ME LAST FOR-
EVER
THEY DON'T COME AND GO WITH THE CHANG-
ING TIMES.
IT DOESN'T MATTER
WHO YOU KNOW, WHERE YOU GO
OR WHERE YOU'VE BEEN
YOU'RE STILL MY REAL FRIEND.

HOW MANY TIMES HAVE YOU AND I
SAT IN SOME ROOM AND LAUGHTED UNTIL
WE CRIED
OVER SOME SILLY SO AND SO
WHO CAME AROUND TO CALL, AND WOULDN'T
GO
AND WHEN I FEEL THE NEED TO BE
WITH SOMEONE WHO'S GONNA BE REAL
WITH ME
IT'S YOU I'VE COME TO DEPEND UPON
CAUSE YOU TELL IT LIKE IT IS, RIGHT TO
THE BONE.

I'VE SEEN YOU GO THROUGH HEART-ACHE,
REJECTED BY THE ONES YOU LOVE.
AND YOU'VE HELPED ME THROUGH TIMES I
KNEW
WHEN I JUST WASN'T STRONG ENOUGH.

SO I WILL ALWAYS BE THERE FOR YOU
COME HELL OR HIGH WATER, RAIN OR SHINE.
I KNOW I HAVE YOUR UNDYING LOVE
AND YOU KNOW THAT YOU HAVE MINE.

AND FRIENDS LIKE YOU AND ME LAST FOR-
EVER
THEY DON'T COME AND GO WITH THE CHANG-
ING TIMES.
IT DOESN'T MATTER WHO YOU KNOW, WHERE
YOU GO
OR WHERE YOU'VE BEEN
YOU'RE STILL MY REAL FRIEND.

Now, as I said, Miss Mahalia takes me back to the dreams and visions of my childhood. And no matter how stressed I get or what anyone says to the contrary, I could feel that I was being carried and that something in me was guiding me along.

Shortest Chapter

Ah, yes.

For all of my past relationships, I have two words and a comment. You've all helped me grow more than you'll ever know; I had to learn to love and honor myself and be happy in or out of a relationship

Another Love

I have never been ashamed of loving someone, but I truly have regretted some of the choices that I have made, or should I say the circumstances that I made those choices. One of the loves of my life was Bob Boogie Bowles, a relationship that lasted 14 years. When I started singing with Jerry Butler, he had a six-piece rhythm section; there were three Black musicians and two white guys. I had seen them on TV, so I knew what they all looked like.

My first job with Jerry was in Detroit, and since I was still working a day job, they decided that they would fly me up there, while the rest of the crew drove from Chicago. Well, when I got to the hotel, no one had arrived except the two guys from Memphis. So I went to my room and decided that I would call them and get acquainted, and Bob answered the phone and there I go again. I loved the sound of his voice. I pictured in my mind that he was the conga player whose name was Bernard, so I said to him, "I really like the way you play the drums. You are the conga player...." He stopped me and said, "No mam, I am the guitar player." I hurried off the phone, because I knew that I was talking to a white boy! Daayum! He sounded like a brother! When I came down to the lobby and everybody gathered to ride over to the gig, I wound up in the car beside him and just looked out the window. I still don't know how it happened, but a couple of months later, Bob was going with me to my ex's, Don's, house to help me get the few items that he told me I could have. Our drummer Gates, who was Bob's best friend, came along to help and laughed his head off telling Bob, "Man, either you crazy or you in love. You goin' to a black man's house on the south side of Chicago to take his furniture out and walk away with his woman." "Well! use to be woman." Don was very cordial and there was no drama. I can't stand drama. I would walk away from drama, but I would fight you, if you mess with my love ones. Another story later.

Bob, Michelle and I later moved to Los Angeles, where we both dove into songwriting with a vengeance. We would stay up all night writing songs, and he was and still is one of the finest musicians anywhere.

He helped me with Michelle and we were happy for a long time. Although, looking back now, I truly regret how I caused pain to someone else. Bob was married when we met, to a beautiful lady. Although, back then, I wanted none of the blame for their separation, I have since matured enough to know that if I had it to do all over again, I would do it different. I was 25 years old and looking for love and validation, as a lot of us do when we're that age. Life sure does teach you though, sometime with hard lessons, but to anyone that I have caused any pain trying to be happy myself, I have learned the lessons and I am truly sorry!

New Chapter

It was Osborne who introduced me to Mr. Ray Charles. He was pretty much the sole writer for Ray now and we decided to write a duet for him. The song was "Strong Everlasting Love" .We also recorded an Osborne song, "CAN YOU LOVE ME LIKE THAT." I love that song! Then we did a remake of "YOU ARE MY SUNSHINE."

I loved working in the studio with Mr. C. Sometimes the engineer Terry Howard would be there, but most times it was Mr. C and me. He knew where everything was and could work the board as well or better than anyone. Wow! Just answered the phone and its Billy Osborne. He is telling me that Terry Howard, Mr. C's engineer, that I just mentioned, has been killed in an auto accident. Got to stop writing for awhile. God bless you Terry.

One day I was in Ray's office, negotiating on some work that I had done, and I was hesitating. I was so broke I did not want to under sell myself and I was scared to death to ask for too much. He says, "Uh, Baby, just tell me what you want, you have done the work, and I am ready to pay you. Listen, Baby, always ask for what you want. Don't ever be afraid to ask for what you want.

So, I blurted out. Fifteen hundred dollars, he reared back and said, "Hell no! I said ask. I didn't say I was gonna give it to you!" But he did! We agreed that I would sign with his label and become his next artist. Mr. Charles said to me "Baby, I have heard many singers, good ones, but you have something special in your voice and I would be honored if you would sing for my record company. I was the one who was honored that he thought so much of my talent. Sadly, Mr. C passed away before we got to sign the contract, but I treasure the duets that we have in the can and I know that they will be released, someday. We had a precious loving, platonic relationship, until he died, and yes he did feel up my arm.

Michelle grew up so beautiful, inside and out. I took her through some changes being an artist. We moved around allot. She went to several schools and traveled when she did not want to. I'm so glad that she is who she is and came to understand me and this dream of mine. She is happily married to Paul, my beautiful Son-in-law and they have brought into this world so much love and talent through my grandsons, Corey and Quinton. My family is my joy! We all laugh allot! You should see us at Lakers games! We all scream! When Barack Obama became president, we all were screaming and crying and my beautiful daughter were trying to explain to her children what this really meant through her tears. We all were a wreck with joy and pride.

Casual Singer

Lord, I spent some time as a wedding, casual singer, with some great singers and musicians, but that is another book in itself. You've seen it on TV, where there is a huge expensive wedding and the band and the singers are in the background, never really heard or seen, but if you stop making music for one second, they motion for you to keep playing. They don't care about your name, your talent, or your special gifts, just keep the music playing. A lot of times, we were on for four hours rotating bathroom breaks. They would serve delicious food spreads that went on forever, but we were served mostly what the band members named bandwiches, sandwiches with a bag of potato chips. I had fun sometimes because I got to work with my best friends, CC Bass, Della Miles, and Theresa Walker. It was the four of us and a few other singers who started upgrading the look of the casual singer by dressing alike, and doing choreography. We all had great personalities, so we had fun for a while until, I found myself feeling disrespected and talked down to, and my memories of the work I had done in the movement would not let me be talked down to!

We were told not to mingle with the guest at all at the casuals, but a lot of time I would see my celebrity friends and we would talk to each other. You can't reprimand me, because I am talking to Smokey, or Jesse, or Maurice White. These are my peeps. One night I did a Beverly Hills Party and, when I arrived, the hostess said to us, under no circumstances that we come across the living room and that we had to go through the servants' quarters. Oooh, that just did something to my insides. I felt as though someone had taken a whip and beat me in front of the whole group. I could not shake the feeling. I did the gig, of course, but I knew I was done with the casuals, although I needed that 300 dollars, I knew I would be taken care of somehow. Oh, don't want to forget this incident before I leave the Casual scene. I was on stage one night during my rendition of Misty, the band was playing beautiful and a gentleman walked up to the stage from among the crowd and stared into my eyes and smiled, listened to the whole song. When I had finished, he shook my hand and said to me, "You are a real talent; I loved what you did with that song. Too bad I could not have found you twenty five years ago." My smile turned into the saddest feeling. He thought that I was too old, although my voice was better than it was at that age. I crumbled, but only for a minute. Then I said to myself, "Self, you are not other people's ideas of who you are. You are who you know you are, keep doing what you do, there is a place for you that only you can fill". That man was one of my heroes, Mr. Dick Clark, Mr. American Bandstand himself.

Mr. Death

I got sick in 1995. I knew that something was wrong, even as I was preparing to do a major concert at the El Rey Theater in Los Angeles. I had lost allot of blood for three weeks which was very unusual. But I knew that I had to get through the show. My friends Jim and Mary Chitty, Reverend OC Smith and Robbie Smith had produced the concert and it was going to be a benefit for OC's church in Culver City, which was my church at that time.

My doctor had told me that I needed an operation, but had scheduled it three weeks after the concert. The concert went great! The band was incredible and my singing vocalists were some of the best in the world. They are my sisters and brother in music, Will Wheaton, Della Miles, and Cynthia Bass. They have always had my back since the day we met. Larry Ball was my Musical Director and always made sure things were popping.

Two days after the concert, I woke up with a stomach ache that would not stop hurting. I called the doctor and she prescribed some drugs that worked only for a little while and the excruciating pain would return. My friends would come over to see me and I would be bent over screaming with pain. The doctor said I only had another week before they would take care of it. I reminded her that I had an IUD lodged in my uterus and she said that they would get all of that out during the operation. By now I was bleeding black thick blood and so weak that I could barley stand up. My friends and Michelle were worried. One night, two days before the operation was to take place, my friends Mary Chittty, Linda Logan, and Robbie Smith's daughter Bonnie came over. Bonnie, who is a nurse, took my vital signs and told my daughter that I could not wait two more days. I had to go to the hospital that night. My blood pressure had dropped to 60 over 52.

They prepped me and took me to the operating room. As I waited for them to put me to sleep, the fear had subsided. I just wanted to feel better.

I woke up hearing a Doctor speaking into a recorder saying, "Patient too infected to do surgery. Have to postpone, and did remove the IUD vaginally."

I was devastated. He did not know I was awake. I wanted to be done. I was crying when they put me in the room and the Oncologist took my hand and said to me, "We could not operate. We had you on the table and I decided to take another look and I am so glad that we did. If we had cut you, you would have died. You have an infection that looks like cancer in the fourth stage, and you are a very sick young lady. We are going to keep you here awhile and give you some killer drugs to try and get you well. Now you will be here for awhile. You won't go home this week or next week, so try to relax."

I know that I was delirious for a few days, because I don't remember half of the people who came to see me. I do remember the night that I could have easily slipped out of this earthly plane. There was no pain anymore; just shallow breathing that took a little effort. I was awake and it was about three clock in the morning. There was a television show on staring all of my favorite singers. I looked up and there was Sam Cook, smiling down at me. There was Dinah Washington, Lavern Baker, Clyde McPhatter, Jackie Wilson, and Sarah Vaughn. They were all singing with close-ups that seemed to peer down at me. At first I was so enjoying the show until it dawned on me that all of these people were dead! I sat up from my bed and said, "Oh no you don't! Not me! Not now! It is not my time!" I thought to myself that if I could stand up on my own, I would live. I pulled my IV tray to me and worked to put my feet on the floor. With time and effort, I managed to stand up. It felt weird. I had not been on my feet for awhile. I then said to myself, "Self, if I can turn around, I will get well!" And so, I turned around. I was determined to see my grandchildren and to dance with my love ones, during this thing called life!

Each day, I became stronger and more determined. I spent a lot of time being grateful and giving thanks. I thank all of the friends who supported me though this time, the ones who came to the hospital, and those who came to see me once I was home.

One day as I was recovering in the hospital, I got a call from my brother, Bobby Womack. Once he knew that I was on the mend, he broke the news to me that my friend Melvin Franklin of the Temptations was also in the hospital on another floor. He said if I could I should go to see him. My sister friend, Della put me in a wheelchair and took me up to where Melvin's wife and family were sitting outside intensive care.

They were not allowing anyone to see him, but they graciously said that I could spend some time with him. Richard Street, another Temptation wheeled me into the room and there he was, the sweetest, gregarious, charming, loving man. He was lying on his side full of tubes and comatose. He sounded like he was snoring, a sound that would become all too familiar to me in just a few months.

Richard said, "You can talk to him Brenda. He will hear you." and I did. I sat there and thanked him for bringing his beautiful gift of music to us all. I thanked him for always being good natured and friendly every time I had the honor of being in his presence. I prayed, I cried, knowing that this would be the last time I would see him on this side of the veil. He now could keep an eye on David, Paul and Eddie!

I left the hospital after two and a half weeks and never went back for the surgery. The big tumor had disappeared and I am healthy today.

Later that year, Michelle and Paul gave birth to my first grandson, Corey. What a joy!

Six weeks after Corey was born, I was standing in my kitchen when the phone rang. Somehow I knew that would be bad, and it was. My sister Mary was on the other end and when she said, "Are you ok?" I knew to brace myself. "Ma'dear had a stroke and is not expected to make it", she said. I sat down and started to cry. My cat, Shadow, began to rub against my legs. She always knew when I was upset. Mary said that she was in a semi-coma and that I should get there as fast as I could. I boarded the plane from LA to Mobile, Alabama and when I got there I went straight to the Mobile Infirmary Hospital with my three sisters. I walked in the room and Ma'dear was lying on her back with her beautiful still black hair up in a ponytail. That ponytail made her look like a little girl. She had bruises all over her body. She looked as if she had been beaten and prodded at every place on her body, except her face. When I asked about the bruises, Mary said that they had drawn blood at dialysis from every place they could, including her neck and legs and that it left those marks. She had a tube down her throat and one in her nose. Then, I heard that familiar sound that I had heard from Melvin, that snoring sound and I knew that she may not wake up. The Doctors told us that her body was shutting down and that it would not be long. That was July 7. The next day would be her birthday. We decided to have somewhat of party, in her hospital room. All of the kids were there, as well as many grandchildren.

We just sat with her and told her that we loved her. We thanked her for all that she had done for us, and then I whispered in her ear that she had done an incredible job with us all. My brother Tim had come from Bosnia, looking so handsome in his Army uniform. She could be proud of all 11 of us, and not one bum in the family. I told her that it was ok for her to go and be with her loved ones who were waiting for her. I told her that we would be alright. We stayed until the nurse told us to leave and the last thing I saw was my Mother grimace in pain as the nurse was taking her temperature. The nurse told me that she still did not like to get her temperature taken.

My high school reunion was also going on and I was to sing at the church for the class of '65 and I did. I sang Precious Lord Take My Hand, hurried home to go to the hospital and when I got to the house; my brother Tim met me at the door.

"Momma passed" I heard the words and although I thought that I had prepared myself for the possibility, my breath gave way as well as my legs. I sank into my brother's arms. I don't think anyone is ever prepared to lose a mother. Even knowing the truth about death and all the Spiritual knowledge that I have learned, this was one of the most painful experiences of my life.

We would lose Daddy three years later, another devastating blow. Daddy was my rock. Even when he got sick, I never saw him stumble or bow his head. Like I said earlier, he was a proud Marine, and walked like one his whole life. My daddy was about six feet one, dark skinned with beautiful white teeth. When I was a little girl, he looked like a dark version of the actor Jeff Chandler.

He had a hard life coming up, losing both his parents as a child and then tossed around by his aunts until he was old enough to go into the service. He fought in the war in Germany and told me some horror

109

stories about the survival situations that he had to endure. He told me about a place for the soldiers called Check Point Charlie that I would visit later when I toured Germany. My daddy would not stop smoking. He did not drink and was very angry that most of his six brothers, including Aunt Gladys, had died because of drinking.

He would not allow even a beer in the house even after we were grown. We used to laugh at Pops. That's what the boys called him because he could talk so much trash, and dare you to tell him that he was wrong. My daddy was never wrong, even when he was. If you wanted an argument, say something that opposed what he said and it was on! He and my Granddaddy would argue all the time and it was a comedy show.

My dad was strict with us as kids, but proud of all of us when we grew up. In his later years, whenever I went home to see him, he would sit on the porch and call his neighbors over and say, "My oldest daughter is home, you know the singer, come and say hello, you know she lives in California." A short time before Daddy passed; I would call him every day, and every day he would be listening to my voice on tapes that I had sent to him of the service at my church or my CDs, but mostly my church tapes. One day when I

110

called, I heard something that I had never heard before. My Daddy was crying like a baby on the phone. Oh, it broke me down. I asked him what was wrong and he could hardly get the words out, he said to me, "Baby, I have not been a good father to my children, I have mistreated each one of you and I have mistreated your mother, I am so sorry for the way I did you all sometimes. Please forgive me. I love my children and I love my wife." I wanted to fall apart and wail at the sound of my strong daddy sounding like a little child almost, but instead I summoned the strength of the God within me to be the one to comfort him, so I spoke softly and clearly and said, "Daddy, we love you, I love you more than words can say, and what I know is that you did the best you could do with what you knew and you knew how to keep your family together even when you were gone sometimes. You knew how to teach us self respect, you knew how to play softball with us when we were young, you knew how to teach us to give more than a hundred percent whenever and whatever job we took on., you taught us to pray, even when you sounded like you were screaming at God when you prayed to make sure He heard you. Yes, you were tough on all of us, and you whipped us sometimes when we thought we did not deserve it, but none of your boys are in prison, you have raised seven, you taught them to be men and take care of their families. You taught them a trade and they all make a living at

111

what you taught them. You taught us girls to be strong and independent, caring, and you sure taught us to love and be there for each other. That is all that matters to any of us; I thank you on behalf of all of us and would not have had any other Dad in this world but you."

When Daddy passed, we had to take his body to Peachtree from Mobile to put him next to Ma'dear. It was so hot that day and to line up all of these cars to travel a hundred miles was difficult. My sister, Mary, was fussing and trying to organize ever one when she blurted, "Yall get in your cars, your Daddy is probably having a fit and fussing right now because folks won't do right." That lightened things up a bit, so we said good bye to our parents and would later let go of our baby brother Willie, at the age of thirty two, from lymphoma. He lived with such joy and humor. He would have us laughing all the time, and could dance his butt off; I know Ma'dear and Daddy laugh all of the time in their Spirit bodies, because they have their baby with them. Oh Lord I miss them all. Our older half brother, Thomas, passed also. He lived with us when we were young then moved to Chicago, some of the younger kids did not get to know him like us older ones. He was Daddy's son, before he married Ma'dear.

Forgiveness and Full Circle

Well I have come to the first half of my life and I continue to write, sing and be grateful. The first half has taught me well. I have discovered the power and the power and the presence of God that it is within me and everywhere in its fullness and that I love and thank God for the Master teacher Jesus who lead the way to the truth that sets one free. I have learned that forgiveness is the key to perfect healing of anything, and I had to do some forgiving. And so, I forgave my third grade teacher who called me Granny, because I was different. I forgave my Daddy's aunts who would bring pretty dresses to my sisters with little pink can slips under them and then bring me a plain dress, no frills at all. Though Daddy did not make a difference, they did. I had to forgive the old white store owner who one day, while Ma'dear was shopping for staples on credit at his store, he pulled me in the back telling her that he was going to try some new shoes on me, then started playing with my little body and looking me straight in

113

the eyes warning me not to tell, and I didn't. The first reason was that I was ashamed, even though I was about nine years old. The second reason was that if I told Daddy, he would have been ready to beat the spit out of that old man and I just knew that the white people would come and take Daddy to jail or something worse. Sso, I kept quiet and my Daddy kept safe. I forgave my ex's, I forgave everything and every-body, but most of all, I learned to forgive me.

And so I have come from behind the starting line to this place, standing in Amazing Grace, ready for the new adventures of my life, ready to live life in love and laughter to be whole and prosperous in every area of my life. To grow and dance in this life with my love ones. I won't stop doing what I do. I will put up "LET GOD BE GOD" again, a full stage production with a great cast of actors, singers, and dancers. "Grace" is the one woman stage play from which this book came from, or vice versa, ha ha ha, "WE WERE THERE" is a stage play with "The Pipperettes" and our time in the movement, and the next one is a musical experience with two other great jazz and blues women , I start writing that tomorrow, so, the best of everything to you and remember, if there is a dream in your heart, a deep desire to do something that you love, do it! It's never too late to live your dream!

LIVE YOUR DREAMS
Lyric, Brenda Lee Eager

PAINT YOUR PICTURE, WRITE YOUR SONG
BUILD A CASTLE OF YOUR OWN
CLIMB YOUR MOUNTAIN YOU CAN SAIL
THE SEVEN SEAS
RIDE YOUR ROCKET SHIP IN SPACE
FIND YOUR QUIET INNER PLACE
TO REVEAL YOUR DESTINY
WHATEVER IT MAY BE

CAUSE YOU KNOW BETTER THAN ANYONE
WHAT YOU WANT FROM THIS LIFE
NEVER LET SOMEONE ELSE TAKE YOUR
DREAMS AWAY
GO FOR WHAT IS RIGHT FOR YOU, ONLY
YOU CAN MAKE YOUR DREAMS COME
TRUE
AND WHEREVER IT TAKES YOU
I'LL BE BY YOUR SIDE

CHORUS

YOU DON'T HAVE TO BE SUPERMAN TO BE
A HERO
YOU DON'T HAVE TO BE AN OVERNIGHT
SUPERSTAR
THE BEST THAT YOU CAN BE
IS GOOD ENOUGH FOR ME
CAUSE ALL OF YOU IS ALL YOU'LL EVER
NEED

115

SO LIVE YOUR DREAMS

OH IMAGINE ANYTHING YOU CAN,
DARE TO FOLLOW YOUR OWN PLAN
TAKE YOUR LIFE INTO YOUR HANDS,
DO WHAT YOU BELIEVE IN.
WALK YOUR OWN WAY DO YOUR DANCE
DARE TO GIVE YOURSELF THE CHANCE
LIFE WILL OPEN UP TO YOU
IT'S YOURS FOR THE TAKING

CAUSE YOU KNOW BETTER THAN ANYONE
WHAT YOU WANT FROM THIS LIFE
NEVER LET SOMEONE ELSE TAKE YOUR
DREAMS AWAY
GO FOR WHAT IS RIGHT FOR YOU
ONLY YOU CAN MAKE YOUR DREAMS
COME TRUE
AND WHEREVER IT TAKES YOU
I'LL BE BY YOUR SIDE

CHORUS

BRIDGE
LET THEM SOAR LIKE AN EAGLE'S WING
LET THEM RISE FROM THE DEPTHS OF
YOUR SOUL
I BELIEVE IN YOU
AND EVERYTHING YOU DO
WITHIN YOU IS THE POWER TO ACHIEVE
SO LIVE YOUR DREAMS

Brenda Lee Eager

Pictorial Portfolio
of
Family and Friends

Brenda & her mother

Brenda the teenager

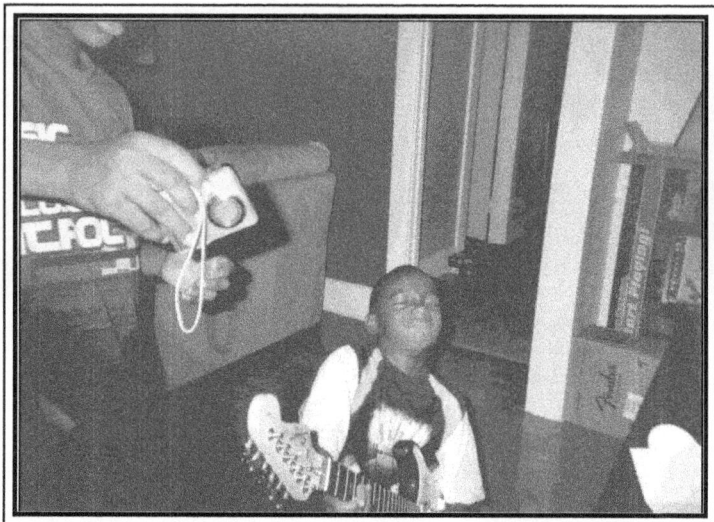

126

132

134

135

Brenda Lee Eager

And T.H.E. Choir
The Heaven on Earth Choir

For Booking Information
Call: (323) 296-9674

The Billy Mitchell Group

Sweet Harmony

141

2 of a Kind
my girl !

145

www.ingramcontent.com/pod-product-compliance
Lightning Source LLC
Chambersburg PA
CBHW030711110426
R18122000001B/R181220PG42736CBX00008B/11